WHY DO I
ITCH?

BY MADELINE TYLER

THE SECRET BOOK COMPANY

©2019
The Secret Book Company
King's Lynn
Norfolk PE30 4LS

A catalogue record for this book is available from the British Library.

ISBN: 978-1-78998-055-4

Written by:
Madeline Tyler

Edited by:
Kirsty Holmes

Designed by:
Danielle Rippengill

IMAGE CREDITS

All images are courtesy of Shutterstock.com, unless otherwise specified. With thanks to Getty Images, Thinkstock Photo and iStockphoto. Front Cover & 1 – Dmitry Natashin, Nadzin, BigMouse, Panda Vector. Images used on every spread – Nadzin, TheFarAwayKingdom. 2 – svtdesign, Anna Violet. 4–6 – Iconic Bestiary. 7 – svtdesign. 8 – and4me. 9 – svtdesign, Anna Violet. 10 & 11 – LOVE YOU, Arcady. 12 – LOVE YOU, marysuperstudio. 13 – Ellika, Macrovector. 14 – Anna Violet, Macrovector. 15 – The Last Word. 16 – hvostik, VectorPot. 17 – Nadzin, BigMouse, Panda Vector. 18 – Rvector, Giamportone. 19 – ann131313. 20 – Giamportone, Jemastock. 21 – Iconic Bestiary, Studio_G. 22 – knahthra, Rvector, hvostik. 23 – ann131313, Anna Violet, Macrovector, Iconic Bestiary.

CONTENTS

Words that look like **this** can be found in the glossary on page 24.

DO YOU FEEL ITCHY?

Have you ever had an itchy feeling on your skin that you really, really needed to scratch?

Some itches make your skin feel very hot.

The itch could be on your arm, your leg, or maybe even your head! Everywhere on our bodies can feel itchy, but why?

WHAT MAKES AN ITCH?

Lots of things can make you itch. Maybe your skin is reacting because you are **allergic** to something. Maybe you spent too long in the sun and now you have sunburn.

Sunburn is red and very painful!

Itches can be very annoying, but they are just our brain's way of helping to keep us healthy and alive!

THE NERVOUS SYSTEM

The nervous system is made up of your brain, **spinal cord**, **receptors** in your skin, and **nerves**. Your skin is made up of three layers: the epidermis, the dermis and the hypodermis.

Hair

Epidermis

Dermis

Hypodermis

Lots of things touch your skin. If your brain thinks something dangerous is on your skin, it will make you want to scratch to get rid of it!

Your skin protects all the things inside your body from invaders!

ITCHES AND SCRATCHES

Start at the bottom of the page to find the source of the scratch!

STEP 5:
...brain, which tells you to...

SCRATCH!

SCRATCH!

SCRATCH!

STEP 4:
...spinal cord, and up to your...

STEP 3: The signal travels through nerves to your...

STEP 1: When something tickly such as a feather touches your hand, it might irritate your skin.

STEP 2: Receptors in your epidermis and dermis send a signal to your brain.

SCRATCH ATTACK

When you scratch an itch, the nerves tell your brain that something is hurting.

This makes your brain think about what is hurting, and not the itch!

Scratching can sometimes make you feel better.

Scratching feels good at first.
But after a while it can make
the itch feel even worse and
might even make you bleed.

Tell the grown-up
who looks after
you if you have a
very bad itch.

DON'T SCRATCH THE RASH!

Sometimes, if your skin is very irritated, you might get a rash. Rashes are often red, bumpy, warm and itchy!

Ouch! Some rashes look like lots of little, red spots.

If you have an itchy rash, try patting it or gently rubbing instead of scratching.

Even though you might really want to, you should never scratch a rash. Scratching can make the rash even itchier, and make it last even longer.

BITING BUGS

Some itches are not just itchy - they're painful too!

Mosquitoes **(SAY: MOSS-KEE-TOES)** are naughty little bugs that leave little bites when they suck your blood.

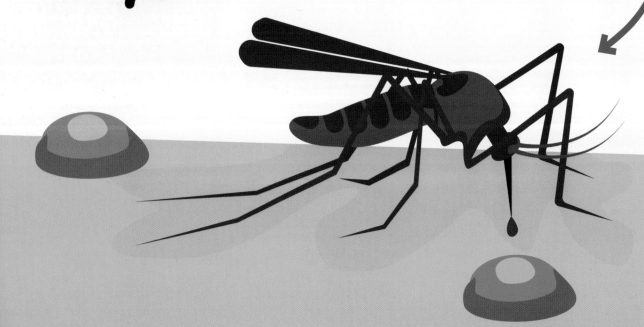

Mosquito bites cause **cells** in your skin to make something called **histamine**. Histamine tells your nerves to send a message to your brain, which then tells you to scratch!

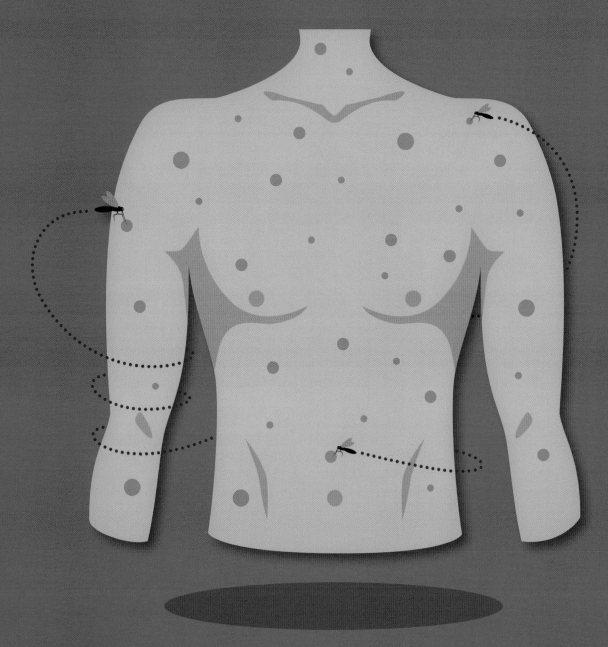

NASTY NETTLES

Have you ever been stung by a stinging nettle? They are covered in hairs that stick in our skin when we touch them.

A nettle sting might feel like you are being stung by loads of tiny bees!

The hairs release **chemicals** into our bodies. This makes our skin red, itchy and **swollen**.

ITCHING REMEDIES

Some itches last longer than others. You might have to use a **remedy** to help.

Some creams for bites and stings have **antihistamines** in them. These stop allergic reactions from taking place.

A wet towel will make your skin feel cooler and less itchy.

Wear loose clothing to keep your skin cool.

MATCH THE SCRATCH!

Which rash is which?
Can you match the itchy, scratchy skin with the cause?

 **Stinging nettle** rashes are red with white bumps.

 **Sunburn** is very red, with peeling skin.

Rashes from an **allergic reaction** all look different. Some have big, red bumps, and others have lots of little, red spots.

 **Mosquito** bites are big, itchy spots.

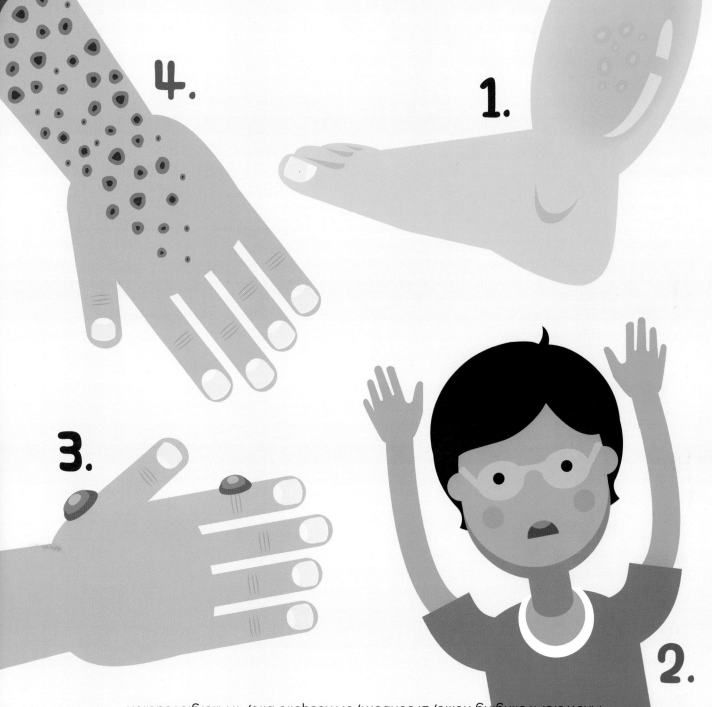

Answers: 1. Stinging nettle; 2. Sunburn; 3. Mosquito bite; 4. Allergic reaction

GLOSSARY

allergic	the body's reaction to an allergen
antihistamines	medicines to stop an allergic reaction
cells	the basic units that make up all living things
chemicals	things that materials are made from
histamine	the chemical produced when the body has an allergic reaction
nerves	white string-like fibres in the body that send messages to the brain
receptors	parts of the body that receive information and transmit messages to other parts of the body
remedy	something that takes away pain or heals a disease
spinal cord	the cord of nerves that extends from the brain and through the backbone
swollen	grown larger or expanded

INDEX